MEDIA LITERACY WORKBOOK

MEDIA LITERACY WORKBOOK

5D MEDIA

5D Media Publishing

Copyright © 2022 by 5D Media

All rights reserved. No part of this book may be reproduced in any manner whatsoever without written permission except in the case of brief quotations embodied in critical articles and reviews.

First Printing, 2022

CONTENTS

Questioning the Media	1
The Power of Comedy in the Media	23
Identifying What is Real	36
The Effect of Media on How We View History	51
Sports and the Media	63
How Much Media is too Much?	71

The exercises in this workbook will teach us how to be a smart consumer of media. We will analyze advertisements, TV shows, movies, and more, figuring out what's real and what's fake.

So why is it important to become media literate? Let's take a look at some of the problems that can happen when we don't know how to tell the difference between reality and fiction. For example, if we're watching a movie and we believe everything that's happening on the screen is real, we might start to act differently in real life. We might think it's okay to behave violently or to do dangerous things because we saw them done safely in a movie.

Or let's say we see an ad for a product and we believe everything in the ad is true. We might go out and buy the product without thinking about whether we really need it or not. In fact, sometimes ads can be really misleading. They can show us pictures of people who are supposedly using the product and make it look like the product is going to make our lives better. But sometimes those pictures are fake, and the people in them are actors who were paid to look happy about the product.

It's really important that we learn how to be smart consumers of media. We need to learn how to think critically about what we see and hear. That way, we can make better decisions about the things we buy and the things we do. Let's get started!

Questioning the Media

To best understand our world you need to learn how to think critically about the messages that are being conveyed by the media. By asking questions about what you see and hear, you will be able to identify bias and propaganda in various types of communication.

The first step is to begin recognizing different kinds of biases and agendas as they appear in popular culture, advertising, education, politics, and more! This lesson will do just that, and introduce you to the basic principles of media literacy.

IMPORTANT QUESTIONS TO ASK YOURSELF:

How do you distinguish a fact from an opinion?
What are the processes involved in creating persuasive messaging?
How does the media portray a particular point of view?
How do you think the media shapes our perceptions?
What are some techniques that the media uses to get us to buy into their messages?
Do you think it is possible for people to be truly objective when reporting the news?
Can we trust what we see and hear in the media?

Lesson 1.1
What Exactly is the Media?

How many types of media can you identify in each of the categories below?

Media Used to Reach a Large Group Of People:	Media Used for Entertainment:
Media Used to Persuade:	**Media Used to Communicate With Others:**

Lesson 1.2
Opinions vs Facts

ANALYZING OPINIONS AND FACTS

When analyzing whether the information given in an advertisement is a fact or simply an opinion, ask yourself these two questions: Is the statement vague or particular? Can the claim be measured or tested somehow? If the statement is vague and cannot be measured, it's likely just an opinion rather than a fact. Be a critical thinker and always do your own research to confirm information before believing it. Here are a few examples.

1) "Our product is the best on the market." - Opinion (O)
2) "Our product has a 99% customer satisfaction rate." - Fact (F)
3) "Using our product will make you happier." - Opinion (O)
4) "Our product has been clinically proven to improve sleep by 40%." - Fact (F)

Understanding these differences will help you to more critically evaluate the claims made in advertisements and other marketing materials. When presented with an advertisement, be sure to look beyond the surface-level claims and investigate the evidence supporting them to determine which statements are facts and which are just opinions.

These distinctions are important for the critical evaluation of marketing claims, as they can help us to distinguish between honest facts and misleading or unsubstantiated opinions. However, it is also important to keep in mind that these distinctions are not always clear-cut, and there may be many factors that influence whether a statement should be considered a fact or an opinion.

Ultimately, the best way to become a critical consumer of advertising is to do your own research and think critically about the claims being made. By following these steps, you can be more confident in the information that you consume and make better decisions based on objective evidence rather than unsubstantiated opinions or marketing hype.

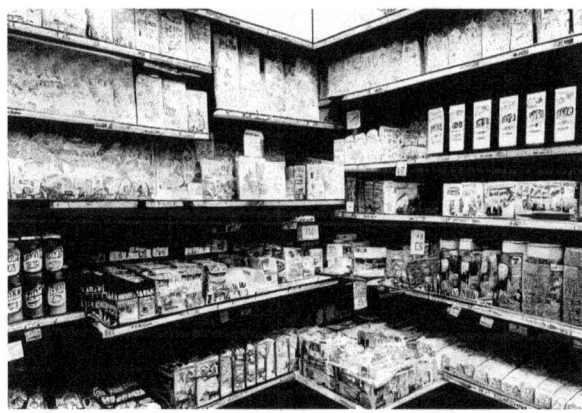

Lesson 1.2b
Opinions vs Facts

Directions: Do your best to label each company advertising slogan below as Fact (F) or Opinion (O). Then, we will review the answers on the next page.

Remember: If the statement is vague and cannot be measured, it's likely just an opinion rather than a fact. Broad claims tend to be opinions, while facts are much more specific and exact. Factual claims can be measured or tested, while opinion claims cannot.

_____ 1. **You aren't fully clean until you're zestfully clean.** (Zest)

_____ 2. **You meet the nicest people on a Honda.** (Honda)

_____ 3. **Wear the world.** (Mondera.com diamond sellers)

_____ 4. **Nobody does it like Sara Lee.** (Sara Lee Desserts)

_____ 5. **For the adult in you. For the kid in you.** (Frosted Mini-Wheats)

_____ 6. **Colgate Platinum. Advanced whitening formula Plus cavity protection, tartar control, and fresh breath.** (Colgate Toothpaste)

_____ 7. **Bet you can't eat just one.** (Lay's Potato chips)

_____ 8. **The ultimate driving machine.** (BMW)

_____ 9. **New Extra Strength Doan's is made for back pan relief.** (Doan's Pills)

_____ 10. **Designed to actively penetrate below the gumline with new dual POWER TIP Bristles and soft, end-rounded bristles.** (Braun Oral-B ULTRA toothbrush)

Lesson 1.2c
Opinions vs Facts

Now it's time to check your answers. Do not worry about getting all of the answers right - instead, focus on developing your critical thinking skills and learning how to distinguish between fact and opinion.

1. **The "You aren't fully clean unless you are zestfully clean" slogan is an opinion (O).** It suggests that we need this product because its better than any other product out there to tell people about how good it really is. A fact would be that soap gets rid of germs.

2. **"You meet the nicest people on a Honda" is an opinion (O).** It is also biased against other car brands; and it conveys the authors view. It suggests that people are nice when they drive Hondas, perhaps because of the reputation and good design of the car. A fact would be that some people buy cars because they like their features while other people buy them based on their reputation.

3. **The "We are the world" Mondera.com slogan is an opinion (O).** It is biased and suggests that people who shop at Mondera.com are more fashionable and cultured than those who don't. This may be true because users can browse through a large inventory of high-quality products, which may indicate that they have more refined tastes than others. But it is still an opinion. A fact would be that online shopping has become very popular in recent years, and Mondera.com sells a variety of jewelry and accessories online.

4. **Nobody does it like Sara Lee is an opinion (O).** It suggests that products from this company are better than every other company. A fact would be that Sara Lee makes a variety of baked goods, which may be one reason why it is successful.

5. **The slogan "For the Adult in you. For the kid in you" for Frosted Mini Wheats is an opinion (O).** It is a personal belief and it might not be shared by all people. It is also a subjective statement because nobody can say for sure that Frosted Mini Wheats are made for the adult and kid in everyone. A face would be that Frosted Mini Wheats are a type of functional food which can provide functional ingredients.

6. **The Colgate slogan advanced whitening formula is a fact (F).** It is using information that can be tested and proven true.

7. **The "bet you can't eat just one" Lays slogan is an opinion (O).** It suggests that many people who eat Lays potato chips can't stop at just one, because they are so tasty and addictive. This may be true but still is an opinion. A fact would be Lays potato chips are a popular snack food.

8. **"The ultimate driving machine" BMW logan is an opinion (O).** It suggests that the BMW brand produces vehicles that are superior in terms of driving performance, compared to other brands. However, this may or may not be true depending on the individual's personal preferences and experiences with cars. A fact is that BMW is a well-known luxury car brand that has produced vehicles for many years.

9. **"New Extra Strength Doan's is made for back pain" slogan is a fact (F).** It is using information that can be tested and proven true.

10. **The Braun Oral B slogan is a fact (F).** It can be proven and tested.

How did you do? Were there any slogans that you were unsure about? What was it that made you question whether the statement in an advertisement was a fact or simply an opinion? Remember, being a critical consumer of advertising requires us to think critically and ask questions about the claims being made. If we are not sure how to evaluate a claim, it is important to do our own research and consider the evidence supporting it before making a decision. Whether you are evaluating an ad for a new product or researching information about a health condition, being a critical consumer of advertising will help you to make more informed decisions based on objective evidence rather than marketing hype.

Remember:

Fact: A statement that can be measured or tested in some way, such as a product's effectiveness or customer satisfaction rate.

Opinion: A vague claim that cannot be readily tested or verified, such as whether using a particular product will make you happier or more successful.

Factors that influence whether a statement is considered a fact or opinion may include things like the source of the information, whether it can be verified by other sources, and the methodology used to support or validate the claim.

Key steps for critically evaluating marketing claims and advertising messages include doing your own research, thinking carefully about the evidence provided, and questioning any statements that seem vague or unsubstantiated. By following these steps, you can become a more informed and critical consumer of advertising.

Lesson 1.3
Analyzing Media Messages

UNDERSTANDING SUBTEXTS, APPEALS AND TARGETS

When it comes to advertising, often the goal is to persuade consumers to buy a product or service. This is done through a variety of methods, but one common way is to appeal to emotions or biases. Advertisers know that if they can get viewers to feel a certain way, they are more likely to act on that feeling. This could be by making them feel happy, excited, or even just curious.

There are many types of appeals, but 3 common ones are testimonials, lifestyle and slice-of-life. Testimonials use personal experiences or endorsements to show how a product or service has had positive effects for others. Lifestyle appeals showcase how using a product or service can enhance one's lifestyle, often by portraying an aspirational image. And slice-of-life appeals show the product being used in everyday situations, with the goal of making it seem like a normal and necessary part of life.

Another technique used in advertising is subtext. This is the implied meaning or purpose of the advertisement. Advertisers often use subtext to persuade viewers to buy their product or service by appealing to their emotions or biases. For example, an ad for a car might not just talk about how great the car is, but might also emphasize how it will make the viewer look cool or stylish.

Advertisers often have a specific target audience in mind when creating their messaging. This could be a certain age group, gender, or even political affiliation. They may also target people who are feeling a certain way, such as insecure or anxious.

Understanding who the advertisers are trying to reach is an important part of decoding the subtext of an advertisement. Once you know who they are targeting, you can start to understand why the ad might be making the appeals that it is. For example, if an ad is targeting young people who are feeling insecure about their appearance, it might use images or slogans that play into those insecurities.

Lesson 1.3b
Analyzing Media Messages

Directions: Identify the type of appeal used (testimonial, lifestyle, slice-of-life), the subtext, and the target audience.

1. We see a young guy and girl playing basketball at the park. The guy makes a crazy shot and the girl cheers him on. The camera switches to a close up of the sneakers as the announcer says "ABC sneakers, for the life you want to live."

The commercial then switches to a montage of different young adults doing fun activities in their ABC sneakers. We see people skiing, snowboarding, skateboarding, and just having a good time. The announcer says "ABC sneakers, for the life you deserve."

At the end of the commercial, we see the guy and girl from the beginning playing basketball again. This time, they're playing at night and it's lit up like a stadium. The announcer says "ABC sneakers, for the life you want."

APPEAL:

SUBTEXT:

TARGET:

---

2. The couple pulls up to a Fast Food Restaurant and they can't wait to have their date night. They're surprised at how busy it is, but they're determined to have a great time. They order their food and they can't believe how delicious it is. They finish their meal and they're so happy that they had a fantastic date night. Thanks to our fast food restaurant, they were able to have a great time without spending too much time or money. Come try out our tasty options for your next date night.

APPEAL:

SUBTEXT:

TARGET:

3. In this commercial, a professional baseball player talks about how his MLB baseball fitted cap fits well and looks good. He continues on about how it makes him feel more confident when he's playing. He encourages viewers to try out a fitted cap for themselves and see how great they are.

APPEAL:

SUBTEXT:

TARGET:

4. In this commercial, you see a group of middle school kids playing on an old PlayStation console that looks like a lot of fun. But then, you switch to a group of friends playing on the new PlayStation console and the graphics are even more realistic, the gameplay is smoother, and they are clearly having an amazing time. The announcer says "That's because the new PlayStation offers the best graphics and technology in the gaming industry. So what are you waiting for? Upgrade to our console and join in on the fun."

APPEAL:

SUBTEXT:

TARGET:

Lesson 1.4
Comparing Media Messaging

RECOGNIZING POINT OF VIEW

Directions: Compare the media messages in the advertisements and news article below.

In an interview for E!'s Daily Pop, Zendaya reflected on her Marvel journey thus far and her uncertain future within the MCU saying, "We were all just absorbing and taking the time to just enjoy the moment, being with each other and being so grateful for that experience."

Zendaya has been playing Peter Parker's classmate and now love interest since 2017's *Spider-Man: Homecoming*. It's an experience that she's shared along with Tom Holland and Jacob Batalon.

In regard to sharing filming three films over a five-year span with the two actors, Zendaya shared, "it's pretty special to have grown up all together."

But with *Spider-Man: No Way Home* now completing a trilogy, it's uncertain whether the three stars' time together in the MCU has come to an end.

According to the actress, "it was so much fun" shooting the third chapter of Marvel's Spidey franchise. However, it was also "kind of bittersweet" since there's no answer whether "we're gonna do another one."

Zendaya continued to comment on the uncertainty further saying, "Is it just gonna be three and done? Like, kind of normally you do three movies and that's pretty much it."

Regardless, the significance of being part of a Spider-Man project and possibly beyond isn't lost on the actress. Having referenced that "there's been so many different Spideys before us," it's of the utmost importance that they're "making everybody proud."

Lesson 1.4b
Comparing Media Messaging

Directions: After reviewing the ads on the previous pages answer the following questions.

1. Who created each message?

2. Who is the target audience of each message?

3. Which message assumes the viewer knows who Zendaya is?

4. How is repetition used?

5. Which message uses vivid verbs to communicate?

6. Which message uses comparison?

7. Circle the words that describe Zendaya's physical appearance rather than her acting ability.

8. Is the purpose of each message to inform, entertain or to persuade?

9. Whose point of view is depicted?

10. What is one fact or point of view that is missing form each message?

Lesson 1.5
Asking Critical Questions

Directions: Watch a television commercial, a scene from a reality show, and a scene from a sitcom. Then answer the questions below.

THE COMMERCIAL

What is the message?

What types of jobs do the creators of this message have?

The main purpose of this message is to (CIRCLE ONE):

TO INFORM   TO PERSUADE   TO ENTERTAIN

SELF-EXPRESSION   TO TEACH   TO MAKE MONEY

What techniques were used to attract and hold your attention?

What point-of-view is represented in this message?

What has been left out of this message?

THE REALITY SHOW

What is the message ?

What types of jobs do the creators of this message have?

The main purpose of this message is to (CIRCLE ONE):

TO INFORM   TO PERSUADE   TO ENTERTAIN

SELF-EXPRESSION   TO TEACH   TO MAKE MONEY

What techniques were used to attract and hold your attention?

What point-of-view is represented in this message?

What has been left out of this message?

THE SITCOM

What is the message ?

What types of jobs do the creators of this message have?

The main purpose of this message is to (CIRCLE ONE):

TO INFORM   TO PERSUADE   TO ENTERTAIN

SELF-EXPRESSION   TO TEACH   TO MAKE MONEY

What techniques were used to attract and hold your attention?

What point-of-view is represented in this message?

What has been left out of this message?

Activity: Locate a media message for a product, event, television show or movie. Draw a picture to represent the message, and answer the following questions: Who crated this message? What is the purpose? What techniques are used to get your attention? What does this messaging mean to you? Who might someone else interpret it differently/ What is the point of view of the message? What information may be missing from the message?

The Power of Comedy in the Media

What makes comedy so important in storytelling? In this lesson, you will learn about the most common comedic characters used throughout history. You will also learn how humor in media has been used to desensitize use to certain situations.

IMPORTANT QUESTIONS TO ASK YOURSELF:

- How is comedy used in media to make a serious point about a social issue?
- What is slapstick humor?
- Why do we laugh at comedic characters?
- How are characters on television and in movies created?

Comedy is often used in media to evoke emotions in viewers. By making people laugh, comedy can create a sense of connection and intimacy between the viewer and the character on screen. It can also help to lighten the mood in difficult or tense situations. In this way, comedy can be used to great effect by those who create various forms of media to achieve certain goals. Whether it is used to entertain, inform, or simply bring a smile to people's faces, comedy continues to be an essential part of the media landscape.

Some examples of how comedy is used in various forms of media include:

- In TV shows and movies, characters are often portrayed as being funny and witty in order to engage viewers emotionally. This can help audiences connect with the characters on screen and make them more relatable.

- In news and current events programming, comedians may be brought in to provide commentary on events or issues as a way of lightening the mood and making these topics more approachable for viewers.

- In social media platforms like YouTube or Instagram, creators often use comedic content such as jokes or parodies in order to draw more views and engagement from their followers.

Overall, comedy is an essential tool for those who work in the media industry, as it allows them to connect with their audiences on a deeper level and reach people in new and interesting ways. Whether it's used for laughs or to help make sense of the world around us, humor will continue to play an important role in how we experience media.

Lesson 2.1
Slapstick

HOW SLAPSTICK COMEDY IS USED IN THE MEDIA

Slapstick comedy relies on physical humor and exaggerated movements. The history of slapstick comedy can be traced back to ancient Greece, where Aristophanes used it in his plays. Slapstick comedy was also popular in Shakespeare's time and was often used it in his comedies.

Slapstick comedy reached its peak in the early 1900s when silent films were popular. Some of the most famous silent film comedians were Charlie Chaplin, Buster Keaton, and Laurel and Hardy. These comedians often used physical humor to get laughs from the audience.

Today, slapstick comedy is still used in media to swap opinions. For example, a news anchor might use a humorous clip from a movie or TV show to lighten the mood during a serious news report. While slapstick comedy may seem like a relic of the past, it is still an important part of our entertainment landscape and continues to influence the way we view humor and laughter.

While slapstick comedy may seem like a trivial way to deal with serious issues, it can often be more effective than straightforward drama. By using humor to desensitize viewers to difficult topics, slapstick comedy allows us to approach uncomfortable subjects with a lighter heart. It can also be used in media to desensitize the audience to a sensitive issue.

In a scene from the movie "Barbershop" Calvin (played by Ice Cube) gets into a fight with a customer and ends up knocking him out cold. This scene is used to lighten the mood and distract from the seriousness of the situation. The issue that slapstick comedy is distracting from in this scene is the serious topic of violence. By using humorous scenes in which characters fight, the movie can address this issue in a light-hearted way. This allows viewers to laugh and enjoy themselves while also learning about the issue of violence.

In a scene from the movie "Soul Plane," the characters are being detained by the TSA and they start to get antsy. So, they start singing and dancing to try and calm down. This scene is used to lighten the mood and distract from the seriousness of the situation. But, when the characters are detained by the TSA, the situation is serious. They are being held against their will and may be facing possible punishment. By using slapstick comedy to lighten the mood, the movie is able to address this serious topic in a humorous way. This allows viewers to laugh and enjoy themselves while also learning about the issue.

Overall, slapstick comedy can be used in cartoons to make light of serious situations. While some may find this type of humor offensive or insensitive, it remains an important part of our entertainment landscape and continues to influence the way we view humor and laughter.

Slapstick comedy can be used to desensitize a sensitive issue by distracting from the seriousness of the situation. In some cases, this type of humor can be offensive or insensitive to certain viewers. However, slapstick comedy remains an important part of our entertainment landscape and continues to influence the way we view humor and laughter. Whether you like it or not, slapstick comedy will always be an important part of our media landscape. So the next time you find yourself watching a movie or TV show that uses this type of humor, remember to keep an open mind and try to appreciate its unique history and influence on our culture.

Slapstick is also often used in cartoons. Some examples can be seen in the cartoon series "The Simpsons" and "Family Guy," where characters like Homer Simpson and Peter Griffin are often the victims of physical humor. These scenes are used to lighten the mood and distract from the seriousness of difficult situations. By using slapstick comedy, these shows are able to address sensitive issues in a humorous way, making light of serious topics for viewers to enjoy. As such, slapstick comedy remains an important part of our entertainment landscape, influencing the way we view humor and laughter today.

Slapstick comedy can be used to desensitize a sensitive issue by distracting from the seriousness of the situation. In some cases, this type of humor can be offensive or insensitive to certain viewers. However, slapstick comedy remains an important part of our entertainment landscape and continues to influence the way we view humor and laughter. Whether you like it or not, slapstick comedy will always be an important part of our media landscape. So the next time you find yourself watching a movie or TV show that uses this type of humor, remember to keep an open mind and try to appreciate its unique history and influence on our culture.

MEDIA LITERACY WORKBOOK — 27

Directions: Read the article below, then answer the questions on the following page.

A BRIEF HISTORY OF SLAPSTICK HUMOR

By Catherine Gourley

He sometimes wears a court jester's hat with bells or a patchwork costume of loud colors. Or the fool may wear baggy-legged trousers, floppy shoes, and a derby too small (or too big) for the head. The fool may not even be human—rather a skinny coyote who pins a sheriff's badge to his furry chest and mail-orders ACME demolition kits and rockets in an attempt to capture the fastest bird in the desert, the Road Runner.

No matter the costume or the prop, the fool has performed buffoonery since the days of the ancient Greeks and Romans. In fact, *buffoon* was the fool's first name.

In ancient Greece, "buffoons" traveled about the countryside, telling stories and playing tricks, cleverly stealing a coin from an unknowing person in the audience. Buffoons also performed in the theater, wearing heavily padded costumes and boisterously boxing each other on the head, belly, and buttocks. The mock violence was exaggerated and silly and apparently very amusing to the ancient Greeks and Romans.

In the 1200s, jesters appeared in England. Many were clever and intelligent, using wit and word play not only to amuse but also to advise kings and other nobility. Some were musicians and acrobats who performed pratfalls and juggling. But other jesters were disabled or deformed and treated cruelly by villagers—ridiculed, prodded, or splatted with rotten fruit. Playing the village idiot often was the only way to earn a meal.

Even so, a widespread belief during these medieval times was that good-humored joking protected a person from misfortune. Jesters, therefore, were good luck pieces who might spread their good fortune to those who were their masters.

Of course if the king were having a bad day or a run of bad luck, he might order the court jester beheaded, according to Daniel Achterman from Princeton University. Was the fool dim-witted or witty? Mocked or the mocker? Read the jest below and decide.

The village idiot provided great amusement to the townsfolk of Coventry. They liked nothing better than bringing every visitor to town to see the fool. They told the visitor to place two coins on the ground before him—a sixpence and a pence. Now, every one knew the sixpence had greater value than the pence. Ah, but the pence was larger in size. The idiot snatched the pence while the townsfolk laughed at his stupidity.

One day, the townsfolk were amusing themselves at this game once again. The newcomer placed the two coins on the ground. As always, the idiot chose the pence. The townsfolk wandered away, still guffawing. The newcomer squatted, stared the idiot in the eyes, and scolded him. "Don't be a fool! The sixpence is worth more! Next time, show them you aren't stupid and choose the sixpence!"

The idiot grinned. "And would I be getting all these pennies if I carried on like that?"

--page 2

Like a Jack-in-the-box, a new kind of fool—and comedy—sprang up in the 1500s during what historians call the Italian Renaissance. (That's just a fancy word for revival of the arts.) The art of comedy, called *Commedia dell'Arte* in Italy, featured two contrasting characters: Harlequin and Pantalone.

Harlequin was poor and stitched his patched tights and tunic from colorful bits of material. He didn't wear the court jester's hat with jingling bells but rather a mask. Harlequin also carried a paddle made of two slats of wood that he pretended to wield as a weapon. The slats slapped together startlingly. It was just more mock violence, however. Like the buffoons and fools who had come before him, Harlequin appeared simple and stupid but really wasn't. His wit—not his slapstick—always got the better of those who were greedy and arrogant.

Pantalone was one of the arrogant. This wealthy merchant constantly looked over his shoulder lest someone rob him of his gold. The old man was a stereotype and no match for Harlequin. Theatergoers of the 1500s loved Harlequin's zany antics and for three hundred years they never tired of watching Pantalone get his comeuppance. Harlequin's character, not to mention his wooden paddle, inspired still another form of comedy in the 1900s . . . *slapstick*.

Slapstick was more than just telling jokes. The humor often developed from an unexpected situation that suddenly arose (also called improvisation), or an ordinary activity that suddenly went wrong.

The Three Stooges bake a cake but Curly gets the ingredients wrong and adds bubble gum—an entire box of gum—to the mixture. In Stooge-fashion, he tries to correct the situation but fails. When the wealthy socialite lady bites into her cake, suddenly—to her embarrassment and the audience's hilarity—she blows bubbles each time she attempts to speak!

Even in slapstick the wealthy, the greedy, the arrogant, and the powerful get their comeuppance—often a cream pie in the face.

Laurel and Hardy, Abbott and Costello, Fatty Arbuckle, and Charlie Chaplin were the masters of slapstick. The costume and the props had changed, but the exaggerated violence and the triumph of the quick-witted underdog—the fool—were still part of the jest.

In 1949, an artist named Chuck Jones created a scrawny cartoon coyote. Wile E. hardly spoke a word but often introduced himself with a business card that read: WILE E. COYOTE, GENIUS. No matter what method he tried—tying a boulder to his feet to gain speed on the Road Runner, painting false tunnels on granite cliffs, strapping himself onto a rocket and lighting the fuse—he failed every time.

So much for genius.

And yet, like the village idiot of Coventry, maybe Wile E. wasn't so stupid after all. Think about it. If he *had* caught the Road Runner, would he still be a cartoon celebrity fifty years later?

1. Who is the "he" referred to in the first sentence of the article?

2. What do you think the author means by "buffoon was the fool's first name"?

3. What medieval superstition surrounded jesters?

4. What character trait do most "fools" share.
    (Greek buffoons, court jesters, village idiots, or cartoon coyote)

5. What is the meaning of the last sentence?

6. What does the story about the village idiot reveal?

Lesson 2.2
Developing Characters

HOW CHARACTERS ARE FORMED

If you want to understand how writers create characters for media, it is necessary to learn the process of characterization. This involves carefully considering the history, culture, and experiences of the character, as well as their personality, motivations, relationships with other characters, and interactions with the world around them.

In comedy writing, it is also important to keep in mind the tone of voice that you want to use. This can help establish a comedic style or tone for your characters by using certain language or humor that is specific to your audience or genre. Whether you are writing for TV, film, theater, or online media platforms like YouTube or podcasts, understanding how to develop characters effectively will help bring stories to life in an authentic and engaging way.

In this exercise, you will invent a character by defining the following characteristics:

Physical Description: At a glance, your character might appear to be an average person, but closer inspection would reveal that they have distinctive features that set them apart. Perhaps they are of African American descent, or perhaps they have a strong build, or perhaps they have unusual hair or eye color. Whatever the case may be, it is important to consider these details as you develop and write your character.

Personality & Motivations: Your character's personality and motivations will help shape their actions and reactions throughout the story. Do they have a playful or mischievous nature? Are they driven by ambition or a desire for revenge? Do they prefer solitude or social interaction? These factors will all impact how your characters navigate conflicts and the world around them.

Thoughts: Along with their personality and motivations, it is important to consider your character's thoughts and innermost feelings. What are they thinking as they encounter a difficult situation or challenge? How do they react when faced with temptation or moral dilemmas? By exploring these questions, you can develop a more nuanced understanding of the complexities of your characters' inner lives.

Setting: In addition to the character themselves, it is also important to consider their surrounding environment and the world in which they live. This can include everything from the physical setting of a story to larger social or political issues that may impact your characters' lives. By paying attention to these details, you can help create a rich and fully realized narrative that engages readers and draws them more deeply into your characters' world.

Behavior: In addition to the other elements that go into character development, it is also important to consider how your characters will behave in different settings. This can include everything from their general demeanor and attitudes to more specific actions like body language or interaction with objects or other characters. By thinking about these details ahead of time, you can help ensure that your character's behavior feels natural and authentic in any context.

Speech: Along with your character's behavior, it is also important to consider how they will speak and interact with others. Are they sarcastic or witty? Do they have a favorite word or catchphrase that they like to use? Whether you are writing dialogue for an individual character or multiple characters, thinking about the different ways in which they might communicate can help strengthen their voice and individuality.

The reaction of others: As your character moves through the world, their behavior and speech will elicit a range of reactions from those around them. Some might find them charming and charismatic, while others may perceive them as rude or arrogant. How others respond to your character will help shape their experiences and relationships throughout the story, so it is essential to consider these nuances as you develop your characters in writing.

Whether you are writing fiction, comedy, drama, or any other genre, having a strong sense of characterization is important. If you want to learn how writers develop truly memorable characters, start by focusing on characterization and all of its many dimensions. As you continue to write about your character, keep in mind all of these different aspects that help shape their development and identity. This will help bring your stories to life in compelling and authentic ways. Explore their history, motivations, thoughts, speech patterns, demeanor, and more. With careful attention to detail and thoughtful consideration of these different factors, you can create memorable and engaging characters that bring your stories to life in vivid and compelling ways.

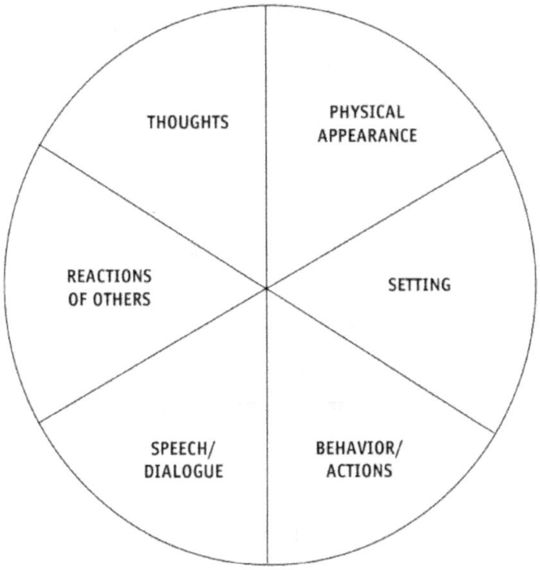

MEDIA LITERACY WORKBOOK — 33

(Wheel diagram with six sections: THOUGHTS, PHYSICAL APPEARANCE, SETTING, BEHAVIOR/ACTIONS, SPEECH/DIALOGUE, REACTIONS OF OTHERS)

Directions: Create a character sketch of a comedic character by outlining the details below.

Physical Description (Describe face, physique, clothing, hands, feet, etc.)

_____

_____

_____

_____

_____

_____

_____

Behavior (Focus on the action and use vivid verbs)

_____

_____

Reaction to others (Who do they interact with? What is their reaction to the character?)

Thoughts (What are their memories? Do they make a wish? What is private about the character that only you know at first, and will make them more relatable?)

Setting (Where are they located and what is it like? Are they at school after everyone has gone home? At home in a city apartment? At a crowded mall?)

_____

_____

_____

_____

_____

_____

_____

Speech (Write a few lines of dialogue)

_____

_____

_____

_____

_____

_____

_____

Identifying What is Real

Media can be a powerful tool for shaping public opinion. It is important to be aware of the ways media can distort or misrepresent events to make informed judgments about the world around us. It is also important to be aware of how media can be used to manipulate our emotions and biases. By understanding how media can deceive us, we can become more critical consumers of information and media.

Media is very powerful and impacts how we understand our world. Music, drama, or other forms of media can shape how we view ourselves and others, as well as influence our attitudes and beliefs.

IMPORTANT QUESTIONS TO ASK YOURSELF

1. Why do different viewers evaluate the realism of a media message differently?

2. What makes a media message seem "realistic" or "unrealistic"?

3. How does the structure of a story affect a reader or a viewer's emotional response, interpretation, and enjoyment of a media message?

MEDIA LITERACY WORKBOOK - 37

Lesson 3.1
Real or Fiction?

WHAT'S REAL?

Media production techniques are used by producers to indicate that a media message is "real" or "authentic." This can involve using certain lighting techniques, editing techniques, or music that is designed to evoke a particular emotional response from the viewer. For example, media producers may use slow-motion or fast-paced action shots in order to add drama and tension to their footage. Additionally, media may be manipulated through selective editing and framing techniques to create the desired narrative or convey a specific message.

It is important to be aware of media manipulation and bias, as this can shape how we see ourselves and others. By critically evaluating media messages, we can become more informed media consumers who can make informed judgments about the world around us. Additionally, by recognizing the media's potential for deception and bias, we can become more resilient to media manipulation and take action to defend ourselves against the media's potential for harm.

Have you ever been tricked into thinking a fictional social media post or tv show was real? If so, you are not alone – media manipulation is a powerful tool that media producers use to create emotional responses and influence our opinions. However, by being aware of media production techniques, we can become more critical media consumers who can think critically about the media messages we consume. So next time you're watching your favorite show or scrolling through social media, pause and ask yourself: is this media message "real" or has it been manipulated to evoke a specific response? Only by recognizing media manipulation can we become more resilient to media deception and take steps to defend ourselves against its potentially harmful effects.

The next activity involves making reality judgments. It is important to understand that reality judgments are different depending on someone's life experiences and exposure to media messages. How someone perceives media has a lot to do with real-world experiences plus experience watching tv, films, and other media. You must also understand why you perceive a media message as "realistic" or "unrealistic."

Some examples of media that may lead to different reality judgments include:

-A popular crime drama, such as Law & Order or CSI, often uses fast-paced editing and dramatic music cues to create a tense atmosphere. For viewers who have witnessed real-life violence, these media messages may seem close to reality. However, for those who have not experienced violence, these media messages may be perceived as unrealistic.

-A popular reality TV show, such as Keeping Up with the Kardashians or The Bachelor, relies heavily on editing and narrative framing to create a fictionalized "reality." For viewers who are unfamiliar with these media worlds, these media messages may seem realistic. However, for media consumers who have exposure to these media worlds, the media messages may seem decidedly unrealistic.

-A breaking news story on social media, such as a video of a police shooting or terrorist attack, will be shared thousands of times. For media consumers who are unfamiliar with these events in real life, these media messages may appear to be real and authentic. However, media consumers who have experienced these events in real life, they may recognize that the media messages are being constructed to evoke a specific emotional response or influence particular beliefs.

Ultimately, media manipulation is a powerful tool that media producers use in order to create strong emotional responses and influence our opinions. By becoming more media literate and critically aware of how media messages are constructed, we can become more resilient media consumers who are better equipped to defend ourselves against media manipulation.

Directions: Watch four different media segments on YouTube, then complete the sentences below. (Suggested Videos: News segment, a fighting scene from a movie or tv show, a trailer for a romantic comedy, a commercial from a home security system.)

Segment 1

This message seems realistic because _____

_____

_____

This message seems unrealistic because _____

_____

_____

Segment 2

This message seems realistic because _____

_____

_____

This message seems unrealistic because _____

_____

_____

Segment 3

This message seems realistic because _____

_____

_____

This message seems unrealistic because _____

_____

_____

Segment 4

This message seems realistic because _____

_____

_____

This message seems unrealistic because _____

_____

_____

Lesson 3.3
Entertaining Reality

THE ENTERTAINMENT VALUE OF REAL EVENTS

Infotainment is a media genre that intentionally blurs the line between news and entertainment to grab viewers' attention. Examples of media that uses infotainment techniques include programs like TMZ, which uses selective editing and fast-paced action shots to craft a "reality" around celebrity gossip, or major news networks such as CNN, which often use dramatic music cues and lighting to create a tense atmosphere during breaking news stories.

While media manipulation can be a powerful tool for media producers, there are ways that we as media consumers can become more media literate and critically aware of how media messages are constructed to defend ourselves against media manipulation. For example, by recognizing the different techniques used in infotainment media or by questioning media sources online, we can become more media-savvy and resilient media consumers.

Directions: Read the TV script excerpts, then answer the questions below.

June 27, 1999, Sunday **FAMILY FOCUS: STUDY EXAMINES TEMPERAMENT OF CHILDREN**	June 25, 1999, Friday **KEEPING THE FAITH: BLOODLESS BRAIN SURGERY PERFORMED**
JANE PAULEY: Many a parent has had dark thoughts at 3:00 AM when the baby's been crying for an hour. But imagine the baby has been crying for days. Other parents may be full of advice, but they never raised your baby. This is not a *Dateline* Survivor Story, but if you've ever struggled with a fussy newborn, you know it could be. Here's Dawn Fratangelo with a *Dateline* Family Focus.	JANE PAULEY: Good evening. Is there anything more important than your health? How about your faith? And what if you had to choose? For the young woman you're about to meet, that was a life-or-death dilemma. Just a teenager, she was desperately ill. There was a medical treatment that could save her life. But it threatened the thing she valued more than life, her religious faith. Chief science correspondent Robert Bazell has our story tonight.

1. A TV teaser is a media message that uses a combination of infotainment techniques such as selective editing and dramatic music to create an engaging and attention-grabbing media experience. In each script on the previous page, circle the words that entice viewers to watch the full episode.

2. News programs are cheaper to produce than fiction dramas, so they use drama techniques to tell nonfiction stories and get similar engagement. What is dramatic or suspenseful about the scripts provided above?

3. News media often pose questions that are meant to keep viewers engaged and encourage them to tune in for more information. What questions are presented to viewers?

4. By focusing on a particular character or event, news programs can engage viewers through suspense and emotional appeals to encourage viewership. Who is the main character and what are the stakes of their decisions?

Lesson 3.4
Historical Fiction

FICTION FILMS BASED ON REAL EVENTS

Historical fiction in film is a media genre that uses dramatic music, dramatic lighting, and narrative framing to create an engaging story based on real-life events. Examples of historical fiction films include *12 Years a Slave*, which tells the story of a free man sold into slavery in the mid-19th century South, and *Lincoln*, which portrays Abraham Lincoln's fight to pass the 13th Amendment and end slavery in the United States.

As media consumers, it is important to be able to critically evaluate the media messages in these films and determine which aspects are real and which have been manipulated for dramatic effect. By recognizing the different techniques used in historical fiction films, we can become more media literate and better equipped to resist media manipulation.

Directions: Review marketing and promotional materials for the movie Liberty Heights. In the space provided, identify what is true and what is fictional. (Note: Truth in historical fiction is often subjective, as media producers may choose to focus on certain aspects of history while downplaying or even completely ignoring others. By paying attention to the narrative framing and emotional appeals used in these media messages, we can learn how to recognize when media manipulation is occurring and make more informed media choices moving forward. In this exercise be sure to focus on what is true knowledge outside of the script.)

1. Press Release

It is Baltimore in 1954 and everything is changing.
In this year, school desegregation is happening for the first time, bringing black and white children from different neighborhoods into the same classrooms.
In this year, the dawning of rock 'n' roll is giving teenagers their first slice of a musical world that will become uniquely their own.
In this year, the influx of automobiles becomes a powerful force in America, allowing people the mobility and privacy to travel at will—to see things right in their own hometowns that were previously unknown to them.
And in this year, the Kurtzman family develops a newly heightened understanding of what it means to be Jewish in a rapidly growing world.

Real:

Fictional:

2. Interviews with Actors

BEN FOSTER (plays Ben Kurtzman): "My character's obsessed with Frank Sinatra, so I got every single album that he recorded from 1940 to 1954. I bought all the *Look* and *Time* magazines from the years 1954 to 1955. The interesting thing is that my character was born before my real-life father was. So I grilled my grandmother about how things were at that time and pored over all her old photo albums."

REBEKAH JOHNSON (plays Sylvia): "Sylvia's father is a doctor and very wealthy. She goes to a high school that is predominantly white and she's one of the lone black girls. Sylvia is just lonely until she meets Ben and then sparks fly. But of course it's forbidden because it is 1954. Her father is furious with her relationship with Ben. Her father considers it disrespectful . . . [the script] says some serious things about race—not just black and white but about Jewish people in the '50s . . . I knew that black people had to sit at the back of the bus but I didn't realize how much anti-Semitism there was."

Real:

Fictional:

3. Interviews about Casting, Props, Costumes and Location

VINCENT PERANIO, Production Designer: "Pennsylvania Avenue was destroyed during the Martin Luther King riots [in 1968] and we only had black-and-white photographs that we researched to reproduce it. We spent quite a bit of time at the Historical Society and I spent five months recalling when I was ten years old, remembering if there were parking meters and what the street 'walk' signs looked like . . . I had a crew of about 35 people working on the exterior neon lights for the old Hippodrome Theater. When we lit up the neon the entire street came alive, with the old cars . . . it was an incredible nostalgic feeling. For three days, this street was back in time and prosperous, and looking beautiful."

GEORGE GILLIAM, Pennsylvania Avenue Commissioner: "During the period of *Liberty Heights*, the Royal Theater on Pennsylvania Avenue was a desegregated area because everyone came to enjoy the world-renowned talent and the artists who played there . . . we've always been proud of the fact that the Royal Theater was a place where we could all come together and enjoy the facility and the social life on the avenue. I put together the band for the James Brown sequence. The casting director looked me up to have me bring my band to have us play behind James Brown in the movie. Me and my committee were very excited about it, because keeping the legacy of the Royal Theater has been our passion . . ."

STEVE WALKER, Propmaster: "There are a lot of little things that the audience will probably not notice that we had to get because the director requested them. A friend of his wore a particular watch that he wanted for the character Trey. It's a Ventura, a very highly collectible watch now and worth thousands, but it was a popular watch at the time."

JOHN STRAWBRIDGE, Casting Director: "For the James Brown concert . . . we had a mass of 500 people. We had to narrow the age range to 18 to 35. And hairstyles today are very different, especially among African-Americans, where shaved hair, braided or dreadlock styles are very popular—none of that would be appropriate for 1954."

True:

Fictional:

Lesson 3.5
Production Concepts

THE VOCABULARY OF THE MOVIE INDUSTRY

Do you recognize any of these terms?

SCRIPT   CONCEPT   RE-ENACTMENT   PRODUCER

SOUND BITES   TREATMENT   GRAPHICS/ANIMATION

TALKING HEAD   B-ROLL   ARCHIVAL FOOTAGE

Directions: Write the terms in the box on the line next to the appropriate definition.

1. _____ Old photos, films, or other visuals used by media producers to provide viewers with a sense of authenticity and historical perspective, especially when depicting major historical events or well-known figures.

2. _____ A media professional responsible for conceiving ideas, finding funding sources, managing production teams, and ensuring that media projects are completed on time and within budget.

3. _____ A written document that contains the descriptions and dialogue for a film or television show, including all necessary information about characters, settings, and plot points.

4. _____ Footage or visuals that are used to accompany media content, often including cutaways and establishing shots. It provides additional context or visual interest, helping media producers tell a more engaging and complete story.

5. _____ A media personality or expert who is often shown onscreen, speaking directly to the camera in a media message. They are typically used to provide expert commentary and analysis about media content, framing media messages through a specific lens or point of view.

6. _____ Computer-generated imagery is used to enhance or convey information that can't be captured using regular film or video images. They can help engage viewers and bring media messages to life.

7. _____ An event that is either recreated or depicted, often using actors or other media professionals. This can help media producers tell a more compelling and engaging story, while also illuminating important historical events and helping viewers understand the significance of those events.

8. _____ A media producer's plan for a film, which includes the story and plot details as well as any necessary information about characters, settings, or other media elements. A media producer will often create one to help them visualize their media project before they start production.

9. _____ An idea or story that is brought to life through media production, including the use of film, video, audio, or other media elements.

10. _____ Used to grab viewers' attention and convey information quickly. They are typically short clips or highlights of a media message, often accompanied by sound effects or other audio cues to heighten the media experience.

Lesson 3.5b
Production Concepts

Check Your Answers:

1. **ARCHIVAL FOOTAGE** is old photos, films, or other visuals used by media producers to provide viewers with a sense of authenticity and historical perspective, especially when depicting major historical events or well-known figures.

2. A **PRODUCTER** is a media professional responsible for conceiving ideas, finding funding sources, managing production teams, and ensuring that media projects are completed on time and within budget.

3. A **SCRIPT** is a written document that contains the descriptions and dialogue for a film or television show, including all necessary information about characters, settings, and plot points.

4. **B-ROLL** is footage or visuals that are used to accompany media content, often including cutaways and establishing shots. It provides additional context or visual interest, helping media producers tell a more engaging and complete story.

5. A **TALKING HEAD** is a media personality or expert who is often shown onscreen, speaking directly to the camera in a media message. They are typically used to provide expert commentary and analysis about media content, framing media messages through a specific lens or point of view.

6. **GRAPHICS/ANIMATION** are computer-generated imagery used to enhance or convey information that can't be captured using regular film or video images. They can help engage viewers and bring media messages to life.

7. A **RE-ENACTMENT** is an event that is either recreated or depicted, often using actors or other media professionals. This can help media producers tell a more compelling and engaging story, while also illuminating important historical events and helping viewers understand the significance of those events.

8. A **TREATMENT** is a media producer's plan for a film, which includes the story and plot details as well as any necessary information about characters, settings, or other media elements. A media producer will often create one to help them visualize their media project before they start production.

9. A **CONCEPT** is an idea or story that is brought to life through media production, including the use of film, video, audio, or other media elements.

10. **SOUND BITES** are used to grab viewers' attention and convey information quickly. They are typically short clips or highlights of a media message, often accompanied by sound effects or other audio cues to heighten the media experience.

The Effect of Media on How We View History

The way we understand history is based on interpretations of letters, photographs, documents, and other forms of media from the past. Historians, writers, and filmmakers provide perspectives of historic events formed by their individual experiences and voice. It is important to understand the purpose and point of view expressed in different forms of media. By analyzing and interpreting these different sources, we can gain a deeper understanding of the past and how it has shaped our present.

As we continue to grow as a society, our understanding of history becomes more complex and nuanced. We are constantly uncovering new forms of media that reveal previously hidden aspects of the past. By engaging with these sources, we can gain a deeper understanding of our history and the forces that have shaped our world today. Through media analysis, we can uncover the voices, perspectives, and experiences of those who lived in the past, giving us new insights into the human experience. And by doing so, we continue to build on our collective knowledge of history and gain a deeper understanding of our past, present, and future.

QUESTIONS TO ASK YOURSELF:

How is our understanding of history shaped by media messages?

How do storytellers help you understand history?

How is the point of view of a writer or filmmaker communicated through various forms of media?

Lesson 4.1
The Civil War

THE BLACK SOLDIERS OF THE CIVIL WAR

In this lesson we will obtain a comprehensive understanding of the role black soldiers played in the Civil War from various media sources, each with its own perspective.

One popular representation is seen in the film "Glory." This film tells the story of the 54th Regiment, an all-black unit that fought for the Union during the Civil War. Through vivid cinematography and compelling storytelling, this film brings history to life by capturing the struggles and triumphs of these brave soldiers.

The book *Lincoln* by Philip Kunhardt, JR. is about the life and presidency of Abraham Lincoln, providing a nuanced perspective on the man who led America through the Civil War. Through extensive research and careful storytelling, this book offers an in-depth look at the events that shaped Lincoln's presidency, from his early political career to his assassination.

The National Archives has provided documentation about Sargent William Carney of New Bedford, MA, one of the few African-American soldiers to receive the Congressional Medal of Honor during the war. An article highlights Carney's heroic actions at Fort Wagner, including his efforts to save a fallen flag despite being wounded multiple times.

Whether through a movie, article or book, historians use different media to portray history in a variety of ways. Each approach has its own strengths, allowing historians to capture different aspects of events and people's experiences. Each also has a different perspective and goal, providing a more complex understanding of history and its effects on people today. By gaining an understanding of how different points of view depict history, we can gain a deeper appreciation for the past and the complex forces that shaped it.

Directions: Review the provided information from each source, then answer questions on the following page.

Synopsis of the Movie "Glory"

During the American Civil War, the Massachusetts Infantry Regiment engages Confederate forces in the bloody Battle of Antietam. Captain Robert Gould Shaw (Matthew Broderick) is injured in the battle and assumed lost, but is found alive by a gravedigger named John Rawlins (Morgan Freeman) and sent to a field hospital. While on medical leave in Boston, Shaw visits his family, and is introduced to former slave and abolitionist, Frederick Douglass (Raymond St. Jacques). Shaw is offered a promotion to the rank of Colonel, and command of the first all-black regiment, the 54th Massachusetts Volunteer Infantry, which will consist solely of black soldiers. He accepts the responsibility, and asks his childhood friend, Major Cabot Forbes (Cary Elwes) to serve as his second-in-command. Their first volunteer soldier is another one of Shaw's friends, a bookish freeman named Thomas Searles (Andre Braugher). Other recruits soon follow, including Rawlins, timid freeman Jupiter Sharts (Jihmi Kennedy), and Silas Trip (Denzel Washington), an escaped slave who is mistrustful of Shaw. Trip instantly clashes with Thomas, and Rawlins must keep the peace.

When the Confederacy issues an order that all black soldiers found in Union uniform will be summarily executed as will their white officers, the opportunity is given to all men in the 54th to take a honorable discharge, but none do. The black soldiers undergo a Draconian training regimen under the harsh supervision of Sgt. Mulcahy (John Finn). Mulcahy comes down particularly hard on Thomas, who has had a relatively easier life than most of squad-mates and is consequently more out of shape. Shaw initially protests the treatment of his friend, but Mulcahy reminds him that this is the same training that all soldiers go through - and as a commander, Shaw has to treat all his men equally. Knowing how badly his men want to fight, Shaw concedes Mulcahy's point. But this causes some tension between him and Forbes, who is skeptical that the 54th will ever be given the opportunity to enter active combat.

When Trip goes AWOL and is caught, Shaw orders him flogged in front of the troops. The scars of his previous beatings as a slave are exposed, presenting a real dilemma for the abolitionist Shaw. While talking to Rawlins, Shaw finds out that Trip had left merely to find suitable shoes to replace his own worn ones. Rawlins shows Shaw how many of the men have horribly infected feet because of their rotting footwear. Shaw realizes that supplies are being denied to his soldiers because of their race. He belligerently confronts the quartermaster, Kendric (Richard Riehle), whom Shaw outranks, and finds out that indeed shoes and socks were in stock but had not been given to the black soldiers. His advocacy on behalf of his soldiers continues through a pay dispute during which the Federal government decided to pay black soldiers less than white soldiers. Trip leads a large protest against the unequal pay and even Shaw himself joins in. The men also receive their Union army uniforms and a new sense of pride is instilled in the regiment.

Once the 54th completes its training, they are transferred under the command of General Charles Garrison Harker (Bob Gunton). Harker pairs the 54th with the 2nd South Carolina Volunteer Infantry Regiment - comprised mostly of freed slaves - commanded by Colonel James Montgomery (Cliff De Young). During their voyage Rawlins is promoted to Sergeant Major. On the way to the main front in South Carolina, the 54th passes through the town of Darien, Georgia, where Montgomery allows his mostly undisciplined unit to loot and destroy the town. When one of Montgomery's men molests a slave servant, Montgomery coldly shoots his own man, blaming the slave's owner as a "secessionist". He then commands Shaw to order his men to burn the town. Shaw initially refuses, citing the order as illegal, but relents under the threat of having his command taken away and his men conscripted to Montgomery. Shaw continues to lobby his superiors to allow his men to join the fight. All their duties since being activated involved building and manual labor.

Shaw confronts Harker and Montgomery and threatens to report the smuggling, looting he has discovered unless Harker orders the 54th into combat. In their first battle on James Island, South Carolina, early success is followed by a bloody confrontation with many casualties. However, due to the fierce fighting of the 54th, the Confederates are beaten and retreat. During the battle, Thomas is wounded but saves Trip, finally earning the respect of the former slave. Shaw extends Thomas an offer to return home for medical leave, but he refuses.

Some time after, General George Strong (Jay O. Sanders) informs Shaw and his superiors of a major campaign to secure a foothold in Charleston Harbor. This will involve assaulting the nearby Morris Island and capturing its impenetrable fortress, Battery Wagner. The fort's only landward approach is via a small strip of beach with little cover, and the first regiment to charge is sure to suffer extremely heavy casualties. Shaw volunteers to have the 54th lead the charge. The night before the battle, the black soldiers conduct a religious service where individual soldiers offer their prayers amid singing hymns. Rawlins and Trip make emotional speeches to inspire the troops and to ask for God's help.

The 54th leads the charge on the fort and heavy casualties ensue on the beach as artillery fire smashes through the ranks. As night falls the bombardment continues and no progress can be made. Shaw attempts to urge the men forward, but is shot several times and killed. Stunned, the soldiers stay where they are until Trip lifts up the flag and rallies the soldiers to continue on. He is shot several times while doing so, but holds up the flag to his last breath. Forbes takes charge of the regiment, and they are able to break through the fort's outer defenses, but find themselves greatly outnumbered once they are inside. Enemy cannons fire at the group of men killing them all (off-camera). The morning after the battle, we see the beach littered with bodies as the Confederate flag is raised over the fort. As the corpses are buried in a mass grave, Shaw and Trip's bodies fall next to each other.

The closing narration reveals that Battery Wagner was never taken by Union forces. However, the sacrifice of the 54th, which lost nearly half its men in the battle, was not in vain, as their bravery inspired the Union to recruit thousands more black men for combat. Their participation would be credited by President Abraham Lincoln as an important factor that enabled the Union to achieve final victory over the Confederacy.

The Book Lincoln by Philip Kunhardt Jr.

Contemplating the heroism of these men [of the 54th], Lincoln was forever changed. He spoke . . . more and more about the black man's earned place in America. "You say you will not fight to free Negroes," he wrote to the Springfield public in hopes of being heard by the whole country. "Some of them seem willing to fight for you . . . but Negroes, like other people, act upon motives. Why should they do anything for us, if we will do nothing for them? If they stake their lives for us, they must be prompted by the strongest motive—even the promise of freedom. And the promise being made, must be kept . . . Peace does not appear so distant as it did . . . And then, there will be some black men who can remember that, with silent tongue, and clenched teeth, and steady eye, and well-poised bayonet, they have helped mankind on to this great consummation . . ."

National Archives and Records Administration Compiled Service Records

Medal of Honor Recipient.

Sergeant William Carney of New Bedford, MA, became the first African American awarded the Medal of Honor for "most distinguished gallantry in action" during the assault on Fort Wagner, South Carolina, on July 18, 1863. After being shot in the thigh, Carney crawled uphill on his knees, bearing the Union flag and urging his troops to follow.

C. | 54 Cold. Mass.

William H. Carney
Sergt., C., 54 Reg' Mass Vol (Colored)

NOTATION.

Book mark: R & P 574 146
with 3632 C.T. 1885.

Record and Pension Office,

WAR DEPARTMENT,

Washington, May 25, 1900.

Medal of Honor awarded May 9, 1900, for most distinguished gallantry in action at Fort Wagner, South Carolina, July 18, 1863.

(438)   Copyist.

C. | 54 (Col'd.) | Mass.

William A. Corner

_____, Co. C, 54 Reg't Mass. Inf. (Col'd).

Appears on

Company Descriptive Book

of the organization named above.

DESCRIPTION.

Age 22 years height 5 feet 9½ inches.

Complexion Black.

Eyes; Black. hair Black.

Where born New Bedford, Massachusetts

Occupation Seaman.

ENLISTMENT.

When Feb. 17, 1863 Mustered in Mar. 30, 1863

Where New Bedford

By whom L. M. Crall ; term 3 y'rs.

Remarks: Discharged for disability June 30, 1864 by order of Maj. Gen. Foster. Promoted to be Sergt. Mar. 30, 1863. Wounded at Wagner July 18, 1863 in hand & hip.

N. F. White.

Lesson 4.1b
The Civil War

THE BLACK SOLDIERS OF THE CIVIL WAR

1. The synopsis of a movie provides a summary of the key events and characters. Who are the main characters in the movie *Glory*?

_____

_____

_____

_____

It is important to understand that the movie *Glory* is historical fiction. The characters Tripp and Rawlins, played by Denzel Washington and Morgan Freeman, were not real people. They were composite characters. A composite character is an imaginary character made up of characteristics of multiple real people.

2. What factual information from the National Archives might have been used to create these characters?

_____

_____

_____

_____

_____

_____

_____

_____

Critics of the movie *Glory* have complained about the interaction of the black characters not being authentic. We cannot fully understand how people interacted during this time period, as much of this information is lost to history. Although *Glory* may not be an entirely accurate portrayal of black soldiers during the Civil War, it can still offer valuable insights into the challenges they faced and the sacrifices they made while fighting for freedom.

3. What might be some of the negative aspects of using historical fiction to portray this particular event in history?

_____

_____

_____

_____

_____

_____

_____

_____

_____

Lesson 4.2
Music in Film

THE INFLUENCE OF MUSIC IN FILM

Music is very important to our lives. It influencers us both consciously and subconsciously. In film and other forms of media, music is used to convey different emotions and feelings. Whether it is hauntingly beautiful melodies accompanying a fairy tale, or rousing military marches in a war film, music can influence the viewers' emotions and help to set the tone for a scene.

Some of the most memorable scenes in film are accompanied by powerful and evocative music. One example is "Schindler's List," directed by Steven Spielberg. The opening scene features an instrumental version of the song "Cry Little Sister," by Gerard McMann, which evokes feelings of sorrow and tragedy. In Disney's "Frozen," for example, an upbeat musical number entitled "Let It Go" is used to express Elsa's happiness at being able to use her ice powers freely. From setting the mood for a dramatic scene, to helping to convey a character's feelings, music is an integral part of any cinematic experience.

Music is especially useful when creating media to depict history because it can evoke strong emotions, help to set the tone or feel of a period and provide texture and nuance that helps to bring the past to life. Different music is used for different purposes.

- Music used to depict fear is often fast-paced with sharp or dissonant harmonies, which create a sense of tension and unease. This can help depict the environmental or political turmoil that often characterizes historical events such as rebellion or social upheaval.

- Music used to depict power and strength can be bold and powerful, with strong percussion or driving rhythms. These qualities help to convey the sense of excitement and momentum that can accompany historical events such as political protests or social movements.

- Music used to depict romance is often soft and sweet, with a lyrical melody and warm harmonies. These qualities can help to evoke a sense of nostalgia or longing that can capture the emotional complexity of historical events such as love stories or family histories.

- Music used to depict sorrow iis often slow and somber, with minor chords. These types of music can help to evoke a sense of heaviness or tragedy, reflecting the emotional complexity of historical events such as war or natural disasters.

MEDIA LITERACY WORKBOOK — 61

Directions: Different instruments are used to communicate emotions. Match the instruments below with the emotions they can best convey.

SORROW | SUSPENSE/FEAR | POWER | ROMANCE

Woodwind instruments (clarinets, flutes) communicate _____ .

String Instruments (cellos, violins violas) communicate _____ .

Brass Instruments (trumpets, trombones, French horns) communicate _____ .

Percussion instruments (timpani, snares) communicate _____ .

Lesson 4.2
History Web

CREATE A HISTORY WEB

A history web is a chronological record of historical events, providing an outline and summary for a particular time period or topic. A good history web is well-researched, accurate, and easy to follow.

Directions: It is your turn to choose a historic event and create your own history web. First, write the name of the event in the circle. Then, add information about the event and how it fits into the larger historical context in the squares. Use your research skills to find relevant media sources to help you build your web.

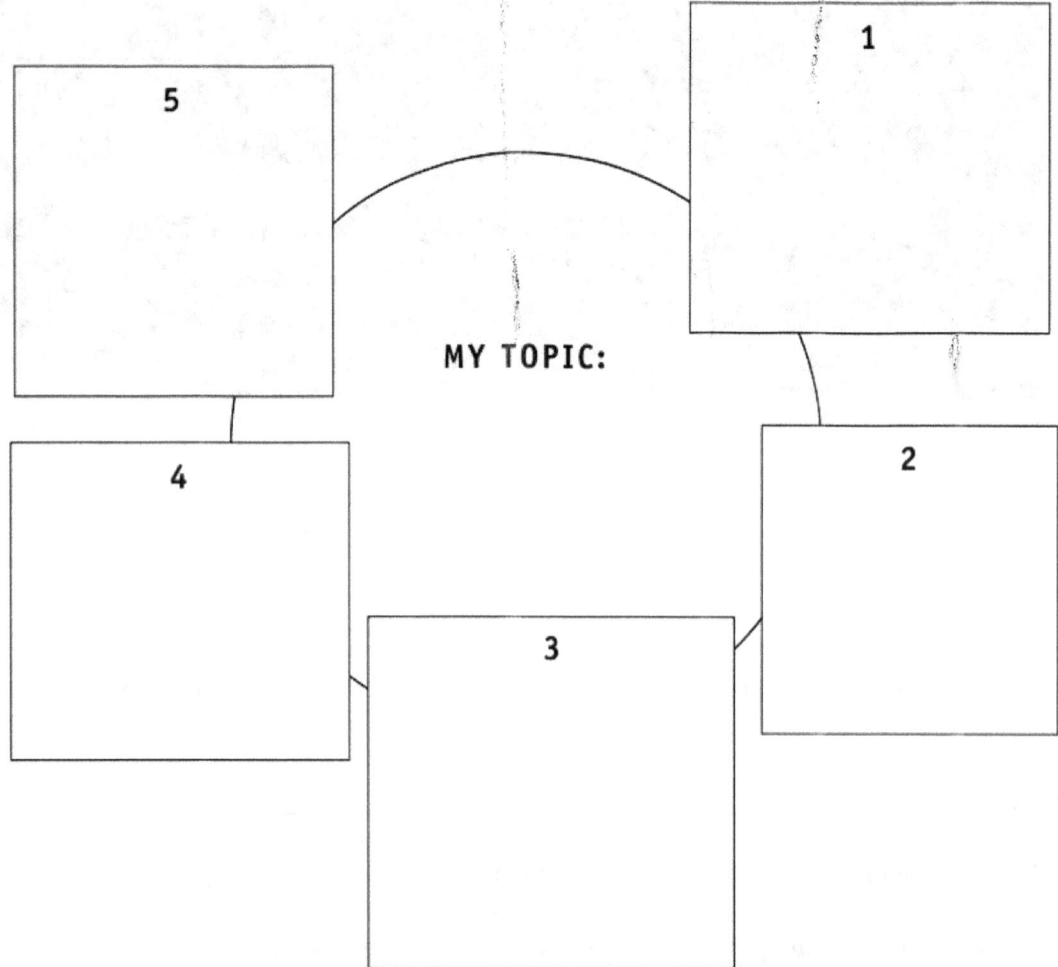

Sports and the Media

Sports have been used as a form of entertainment throughout recorded history. Unfortunately, violence, gender roles, and stereotyping often play a role in how these events are portrayed by the media. This chapter discusses the symbolic violence of sports and how it is used by the mass media to reinforce harmful messages about gender, race, and social class.

It is important to be aware of these dynamics so that we can question the way sports are presented to us and critique the broader implications of these images and messages.

Questions to Ask Yourself

How are professional athletes now similar to those of the past?

Why do people like watching sports and what impact does it have on values, beliefs, and behaviors?

How are gender stereotypes reenforced or altered through broadcast sports, and what impact do they have on viewers?

Lesson 5.1
Sports Messaging

THE UNDERLYING MESSAGING IN SPORTS MEDIA

The mass media has a powerful influence on how we view sports and the athletes involved. For example, the media often highlights violent play or the use of physical force by players, reinforcing harmful stereotypes about masculinity and violence. While women athletes are often depicted in stereotypical ways, such as being submissive or sexualized.

At the same time, the media can also reinforce harmful gender, racial, and class stereotypes through the portrayal of athletes and sports. For example, it is not uncommon to see images of hyper-masculine black male athletes who are portrayed as being aggressive and violent.

In order to critically engage with these representations, it is important to be aware of the broader implications of these messages. We need to question the way sports are presented to us and actively challenge the ways in which these images and messages reinforce harmful stereotypes about gender, race, and social class. By doing so, we can work towards a more inclusive and equitable society that truly values all people, regardless of their race, gender identity, or socioeconomic status.

Directions: Answer the questions below as thoroughly and honestly as possible.

1. What are some of the ways sports are portrayed in the media?

_____
_____
_____
_____
_____

2. Why is it important to be aware of these dynamics when it comes to sports and media coverage?

3. How do you think these negative portrayals of sports might impact society as a whole?

_____
_____
_____
_____
_____
_____
_____
_____
_____
_____
_____
_____
_____
_____

4. What can we do to challenge and resist these harmful messages about sports in the media?

_____
_____

There is no single answer to these questions, as the dynamics surrounding sports and the media are complex and multifaceted. Some potential approaches might include reading and researching more about how gender, race, and social class are portrayed in the media, and speaking with others who also question media messages.

Each of us experiences some sort of emotional response when it comes to sports. This makes sports ideal for media representation and manipulation. We love, hate, admire and criticize sports, but what is the underlying reason behind our response to these events? Wrestling is one example of a sport that is often associated with violence and stereotyping in mass media. It is well-known for its exaggerated displays of aggression, and this can reinforce harmful messages .

Lesson 5.2
Violence in Sports

THE DARK SIDE OF SPORTS

Gladiator fighting was a popular form of entertainment in Ancient Rome. It involved two combatants fighting each other in an arena and often resulted in serious injury or death. Gladiator fighting was considered to be very exciting and entertaining, and it drew large crowds of spectators. The fighters were usually slaves or prisoners who were forced to fight for the amusement of the crowd.

While wrestling and football may not seem as brutal as gladiator fighting, the underlying messages conveyed through these sports are still problematic. In particular, both sports rely on exaggerated displays of aggression and violence in order to entertain fans. This can be extremely harmful, as it reinforces harmful stereotypes about masculinity and violence.

At the same time, it is important to note that there are some differences between modern-day wrestling and football and their gladiator predecessors. For example, football is far more lucrative and popular than gladiator fighting ever was, and the athletes in this sport are much better compensated. Additionally, wrestling has become more "family-friendly" over the years, which means that there is less emphasis on violence and bloodshed. Despite these differences, it is clear that both wrestling and football are still deeply rooted in a culture of violence and aggression. And until we start to question the way these events are portrayed in mass media, we will continue to see the negative consequences of these stereotypes play out in society as a whole.

Directions: Read the article and then answer the questions that follow.

RAGE IN A CAGE

By Catherine Gourley
Excerpted from *Media Wizards*

When Joanie was a little girl growing up in Rochester, New York, her brothers used to wrestle inside the dog kennel in the backyard. In these cage matches, the boys imitated the TV stars of the World Wrestling Federation (WWF). Joanie loved sports, all kinds of sports. The only way she could join the boys' game was not by practicing her hammerlock but by making championship belts out of tinfoil for whoever won the match inside the dog cage.

That was one of Joanie's lives. Graduating with honors from high school and studying Spanish literature at the University of Tampa, Florida, was her other life. Joanie's dream was to work for the Peace Corps or join the Secret Service as an agent. You might say her dream came true. Joanie has gone undercover as "Chyna," only it's not the United States government she is protecting. It's the WWF's DeGeneration-X, a team of professional wrestlers.

When Chyna strides calmly into an arena—wearing a sleeveless black leather vest, black boots, and black shades—the fans take notice. So do the wrestlers in the ring. Chyna commands respect, in part because her body is so incredibly powerful, but also in part because she is so coolly self-controlled. She doesn't smile. She rarely speaks. Fans may jeer at her, but she never cracks. She's there to do a job: protect DX superstars Shawn "The Heartbreak Kid" Michaels, the Road Dog, and X-Pac. No one wrestles dirty and gets away with it when Chyna is in the house.

It's all an act, though. The WWF is a game, not so different really than a bunch of kids wrestling in the backyard. Well, maybe a little different. Now Joanie wrestles instead of fashioning tinfoil belts for the boys. And she does it in front of millions of fans and TV viewers. Now it isn't stupid. Now it's very profitable and, she admits, even thrilling.

What's real and what's fake about world wrestling?

For one thing, the money is real. Fans spend millions, and not just on tickets for the explosive live events. Spending doesn't stop at ringside, either. The wrestling federation has licensed a magazine and video games, not to mention T-shirts, hats, gym bags, drinking cups, wristwatches, backpacks, cardboard stand-ups of WWF stars . . . even beach blankets!

The wrestling is also real. Those scoop slams to the mat and double clotheslines over the ropes are choreographed and practiced as in any sport, but they are crunchingly right on. Yet even the wrestlers themselves admit it's pure entertainment. "Basically, we are all human versions of superheroes," says Mike "The Hitman" Hart. He compares himself to Batman. "Only I'm a little better," he adds.

Within a year of joining the federation, Chyna had been dubbed "the fourth wonder of the world" and became a comic book superhero in her own right—the Amazon, the woman warrior. Still, in portraying Chyna, Joanie has also broken a stereotype—the one that says girls don't belong in the sport of wrestling.

"Right now, I'm working with the guys on their level," she says.

Joanie describes Chyna as if she is someone other than herself. "There's a mystery to Chyna. You never see her jumping up and down or really smiling. There is so much I can do with my character. She hasn't even been unleashed yet."

1. Beyond televised performances, what other media does the World Wrestling Federation use to promote its stars and matches?

2. Joanie calls Chyna "her character." The methods of characterization used by fiction writers include passages of written text describing the character's physical appearance, behavior or actions, thoughts, dialogue, and the reaction of others. Which methods of characterization does Joanie use to create Chyna? Provide examples.

3. In creating this article, the author selected quotes by Joanie and Mike "The Hitman" Hart.

    a. What does Hart want you to believe about professional wrestlers?

    b. What does Joanie want you to believe about Chyna?

    c. What does the author of this article want you to believe about the World Wrestling Federation?

4. The author compares Chyna to an Amazon. Who were the Amazons? Is this or is this not an appropriate comparison? Why?

5. The author explains some of the things about wrestling that are real. What aspects of wrestling are not real?

How Much Media is too Much?

Media consumption has a lasting effect on you. Different types of media can enlighten, change, and shape your perspective. It's important to be aware of how much you are consuming so you can better control what sort of an impact it will have on your life.

Media has always been a powerful tool for spreading ideas and influencing change. From the colonial newspapers in Great Britain heralding their dominance over the world to Nazi propaganda representing a new "master race", media has been used to express ideas and influence behavior for hundreds of years. Today, we are inundated with media from all angles – social media accounts, news websites, big media networks, and more. With this abundance of media, it is easy to lose track of what you are consuming and how it's affecting you.

Before blindly accepting the messages that we receive from various sources, it is important to recognize the impact media can have on you and your life. Different types of media can enlighten us about the world around us, spark change in beliefs and ideologies, or reinforce unhelpful habits. This leads to a more informed population with a greater understanding of the world around them – an ideal outcome for any society.

On the other hand, if you are consuming too much media, it can create negative effects on your life. For example, research has shown that heavy media use can lead to depression and anxiety. Additionally, the content of media may be detrimental – for example, if you consume a lot of violent TV or video games, it could stimulate aggressive behavior in real life.

Taking this into account, it is important to monitor your own media consumption so that you are aware of the effects it is having on you. If you notice that a particular source or type of content is negatively affecting your life, try to find alternative media sources and types of content – you may be surprised by how much more positively your outlook changes as a result!

Media consumption has both positive and negative effects on you and your life. By paying attention to how much media you consume and what that content is, you can stay informed about the world around you while avoiding negative consequences on your mental health or behavior.

Questions to Ask Yourself

How much media do you consume?

Can media affect your relationships with your family members and friends?

Can media be addictive?

Lesson 6.1
Media Consumption

ANALYZE THE AMOUNT OF MEDIA YOU CONSUME

In this exercise, we will analyze your personal media consumption behaviors. It is important to be mindful of the amount of media we consume, as there can be both positive and negative effects. Some possible benefits of consuming media include being more informed about the world around us and staying up-to-date on current events. However, too much media consumption can lead to negative effects such as depression or aggressive behavior. To start, it is helpful to take stock of your existing media habits.

What are your media consumption behaviors? Do you find yourself mindlessly scrolling through social media, or do you actively seek out new content to engage with? What role does media consumption play in your life and relationships? Are there any specific sources of media that have a particularly strong impact on you? Ultimately, the goal is to become more mindful of our personal media consumption habits. By paying attention to the ways that media affects us and our lives, we can better understand its role in our lives and make informed choices about how much and what types of content we engage with.

Directions: Answer the questions below to analyze your media consumption behaviors.

1. Watching TV helps me forget about stressful things in my life   True   False (circle one)

2. I spend _____ hours every _____ on social media.

3. I watch violent TV shows and movies (Frequently / Sometimes / Never).

4. How much media do you consume every day? _____
_____

5. What types of media do you consume? _____

_____

_____

6. What are the effects of that media on your life?

_____

_____

_____

_____

_____

_____

7. Review your answers. What does this say about your media consumption behaviors?

_____

_____

_____

_____

_____

_____

**Lesson 6.2
Final Analysis**

YOUR ATTITUDE ABOUT MEDIA CONSUMPTION

Your attitude about your media consumption is just as important as your behavior. In order to optimize your media consumption, it is important to be aware of both its positive and negative effects. To start, you might consider tracking how much time you spend consuming media each day as well as the content you engage with as you did in the previous exercise. This can help you identify any problematic habits or patterns, and allow you to make changes accordingly.

Additionally, you might consider discussing your media consumption habits with family members or friends, to compare your experiences and gain a better understanding of how others are affected by media. Finally, it is important to be mindful of the various sources of media that influence you - social media platforms, news outlets, or other types of content. By becoming more aware of these influences, you can make more informed choices about how and when you engage with media.

Directions: Answer the questions below to analyze your attitude about media consumption.

1. If you go on vacation and can only bring one form of media, what would it be? _____

2. Most celebrities deserve fame.   True   False   (circle one)

3. I like listing to music while doing my homework.   True   False   (circle one)

4. People who create TV shows only care about money.   True   False   (circle one)

5. Do you think you consume too much or too little media? _____

6. Do you feel that too much media can lead to negative consequences?

_____

_____

_____

_____

_____

_____

7. How does your own personal media consumption compare with that of your friends and family members?

_____

_____

_____

_____

_____

_____

8. Based on your answers above, what is your attitude about media consumption?

_____

_____

_____

_____

_____

_____

9. What changes should you make in the future?

_____

_____

_____

_____

_____

Now that you have completed this workbook, you should be familiar with the basics of media literacy. You know how to identify different types of media, analyze their messages, and think critically about the effects they have on your life. You also understand the importance of being a savvy consumer of information and how to find accurate sources of news and information.

We hope that you will continue to explore these topics and practice your skills as you become more proficient in media literacy. As always, if you have any questions or need help navigating these concepts, don't hesitate to reach out to us for support.

www.ingramcontent.com/pod-product-compliance
Lightning Source LLC
Chambersburg PA
CBHW081711100526
44590CB00022B/3734